# Rouen

Text Henry Decaëns
Photography Éric Pouhier
Translation id2m



**Front cover.**
The cathedral seen from the belfry of the *Gros-Horloge.*

**Back cover.**
View of Rouen from the top of Sainte-Catherine Hill.

**Inset, from left to right.**
Dial of the *Gros-Horloge* (16th century).
Half-timbered houses, Rue Saint-Romain.
Saint-Ouen Church, 14th-century stained glass window: the Annunciation.

**Left-hand page.**
Church of Sainte-Jeanne d'Arc, vitrail des Chars or 'Triumph of the Virgin' stained glass window, crafted by Engrand and Jean le Prince between 1522 and 1524.

Editions OUEST-FRANCE

1.

1.
The cathedral seen from the crossing tower of Saint-Ouen Church.

2.
The Seine at Lacroix Island.

3.
Rue du Petit-Mouton.
The red half-timbered house is one of the oldest in Rouen (13th century) and used to be home to an inn where Simone de Beauvoir and Jean-Paul Sartre lived between 1934 and 1936 while they were teachers in Rouen and Le Havre.

## A Provincial City

The City of Rouen is located 75 miles from the sea, at the top of a loop in the River Seine. The amphitheatre of hills which rises above the northern part of the city is interrupted by the valleys carved by the Cailly and Robec rivers. Early inhabitants settled on a plateau between these two tributaries of the Seine where their homes were sheltered from the river's flooding.

The effects of the tide, a considerable advantage for shipping, are still in evidence, and it is hardly surprising that people have long been drawn to this site for trading. The Gallic name for the city, *Ratumacos*, apparently meant 'trading centre'.

In the late third century the city became the capital of a Roman administrative district known as the *Seconde Lyonnaise*. From the early fourth century onwards it was the seat of a bishopric, where St. Romain and St. Ouen would later gain fame in the seventh century. Promoted

2.

## Half-timbered houses

The vast forests which still surround Rouen today provided the oak needed for house-building from the Gallo-Roman era to the 19th century. The oldest and most picturesque of the two thousand half-timbered houses which can still be found in Rouen are corbelled: in order to save space in these houses, which generally only had one room per floor, each level was built to overhang the floor below. It is easy to imagine the problems that this caused in very narrow streets; in an effort to clean up the city, corbelling was therefore banned in Rouen in 1520.

Rue du Gros-Horloge, Rue Saint-Romain, Rue Martainville, Rue Damiette and Rue Eau-de-Robec are lined with half-timbered houses from various eras. Some of these houses have been repainted in recent years in what is believed to be their original colours.

to the status of archbishopric in the mid-eighth century, it was pillaged by the Vikings and was the only important town in the territory to be surrendered in 911 by the King of France, Charles the Simple, to the Viking leader Rollo, the first Duke of Normandy – the land of the people of the North.

The Dukes of Normandy established one of their main places of residence in Rouen; like its counterpart in London, this was known as the *Tower*. They were crowned in the cathedral, where several Norman princes are also buried, including the first two, Rollo and his son William Longsword.

Rouen's port enabled it to become a major trading centre. A busy industrial centre also developed near the rivers: drapers, fullers and dyers set up on the Robec and Aubette rivers and tanners close to the River Renelle. Between 1160 and 1170, the middle classes obtained a communal charter, known as the *Etablissements de Rouen*, which allowed them to manage their own affairs.

3.

1.

# France's Second City (13th-16th Century)

The annexation of Normandy to France in 1204 did not alter the city's status; Philip Augustus confirmed its rights and privileges. After having ordered the destruction of the city walls and the Tower, however, he reaffirmed his presence by building a royal residence, Bouvreuil Castle. All that remains of the castle today is the keep, known as the Joan of Arc Tower.

The traditional trade links with England were not severed and the 13th century proved to be particularly prosperous. At that time, Rouen numbered between 30,000 and 40,000 inhabitants and was France's second city, a status it would maintain until the end of the 16th century.

In the early 14th century, a major royal arsenal, the *Clos aux Galées*, was built on the left bank of the Seine. The Exchequer, the itinerant Norman feudal court, was permanently established in Rouen during the same period.

The city was not spared from the misfortunes of the times, however, suffering during the Hundred Years War and facing epidemics of the plague in 1348 and 1379 and floods in 1373 and 1382. Burdened with heavy taxes, the inhabitants rebelled on several occasions; the most well-known uprising, the 'Harelle' revolt in 1382, was brutally quashed by King Charles VI, who abolished the office of Mayor.

In 1419, after a six-month siege, the people of Rouen surrendered to the English, who would occupy the city until 1449.

After the Hundred Years War, the city once again experienced a period of prosperity which would last for over a century. It housed all the legal and administrative institutions of a provincial capital, chief among which was the Exchequer, transformed into a *Parlement* in 1515.

## Some of Rouen's famous inhabitants

Rouen was the birthplace of numerous celebrities, only a handful of whom can be mentioned here:

– literary masters, including the author of Le Cid, **Pierre Corneille** (1606-1684), who was born and lived a stone's throw from Place du Vieux Marché; his nephew, **Fontenelle** (1657-1757); **Gustave Flaubert** (1821-1880), who wrote most of his works, including Madame Bovary, in Croisset, close to Rouen; and **Maurice Leblanc** (1864-1941), father of the famous Arsène Lupin.

– Talented painters including **Jean Letellier** (1614-1676), **Jean Jouvenet** (1647-1717), **Jean Restout** (1692-1768) and **Théodore Géricault** (1791-1824).

– Musicians, including **François Boieldieu** (1775-1834), master of the comic opera, and **Marcel Dupré** (1886-1971), composer of several works for organ.

– Finally, mention must be made of the explorer **Cavelier de La Salle** (1643-1687), who led an exhibition down the Mississippi River and founded Louisiana; the biologist **Charles Nicolle** (1866-1936), winner of the Nobel Prize in Medicine in 1928 for his discoveries on the transmission of typhus; the naturalist **Théodore Monod** (1902-2000); and the film director **Jacques Rivette**.

2.

3.

1.
Bouvreuil district and the castle keep built by Philip Augustus in the early 13th century.

2.
Detail of the tympanum over the Saint-Jean entrance to the cathedral: Herod's feast, the dance of Salome and the beheading of St. John the Baptist (early 13th century).

3.
Ambulatory of the cathedral: head of the tomb of William Longsword (14th century).

4.
Church of Sainte-Jeanne d'Arc, *vitrail des Chars* or 'Triumph of the Virgin' stained glass window (16th century): the oldest representation of the stone bridge across the Seine from the 12th to the early 17th century.

4.

1.

1.
*Hôtel-Dieu* (17th-18th century),
home to the region's prefecture since 1995.

2.
Half-timbered houses from the 17th
and 18th century in Rue des Faulx,
to the south of Saint-Ouen Church.

## Developments in the Modern Era

Peace was shattered during the second half of the 16th century by the Wars of Religion. The following century, the city experienced a period of recession; however, prosperity returned in the 18th century thanks to the cotton industry, which replaced the wool industry, and to earthenware.

The city's appearance began to change: the mediaeval city walls were taken down before the French Revolution and wide boulevards were built in the place of ditches.

In the 19th century, traffic using the city's port increased and industry sprang up along the left bank of the Seine. New roads were laid across the city's mediaeval fabric, leading to the destruction of some monuments and several houses; however, these losses were minor in comparison with those sustained during the Second World War.

2.

## The port

Rouen is both a river and sea port, located 75 miles from the sea and from Paris. With 23 million tonnes of goods per year, it is the fifth largest port in France. It receives between 3,500 and 4,500 ships each year; the largest are almost 300m long and have a deadweight of around 160 000 tonnes.
The port is the European Union's largest exporter of cereals and has silos which constitute more than half of France's storage capacity for cereals. It also has specialist terminals for the transit of cereals, flour and sugar.
Rouen is also France's main port for flour exports, for the agrifood sector and agro-industry, and for fertilisers, malt and paper products. It is France's second-largest port for sugar, the third-largest for conventional goods, wood and oil products and the fourth-largest for containers. Most of the traffic is bulk goods: either liquids, such as refined oil products, or solids, such as cereals.
The independent port of Rouen also plays a major role in the economic development of the Lower Seine.

3.

On the right bank, the town planner in charge of the city's reconstruction respected the former urban layout. On the left bank, however, the war had wiped out the past and a modern district was able to be built.

Today, the city itself has 108,000 inhabitants and is at the centre of an urban area four times the size. It has been the capital of the *Haute-Normandie* (Upper Normandy) region since its creation in 1964.

4.

3.
Rouen port,
the sugar terminal.

4.
Madonna with Child decoration on a post in a 16th-century house on Place du Lieutenant-Aubert.

1.

1.
The west façade of the cathedral.

2.
The cathedral seen from
the chancel of Saint-Ouen.

3.
The south side of the cathedral;
in the foreground, the building housing
the revestiary and the cartulary (13th century).

## The Outside of Notre-Dame Cathedral

Rouen Cathedral is a complex monument which bears witness to the entire development of Gothic architecture. All that is left of the previous 11th-century building are the remains of its crypt. Work on the current cathedral began in around 1150 with the construction of Saint-Romain Tower; the façade was begun in 1170, the nave in 1185 and the transept and the chancel followed. The cathedral was finished in around 1240 but continued to undergo both minor and major changes until the early 16th century. The resulting lack of unity, striking from the west façade, is one of the cathedral's most attractive features.

This **façade**, whose construction spanned the period from the 12th to the 16th century, was immortalised in some thirty paintings by Claude Monet in 1892 and 1893. It is unusually wide (61 m) because the side towers stand to each side of the building. On the left is Saint-Romain Tower; this dates from the mid-12th century, apart from its top level, added in the 15th century. Its simple lines contrast with the rich decoration of Butter Tower (1488-1506), on the right, which is characteristic of the Flamboyant Gothic style. The name of this tower does not merely refer to the ochre colour of its stone but also to the fact that it was built with the alms money given by members of the congregation in exchange for the right to eat butter during Lent!

The jambs and arch mouldings on the side porches, completed in around 1200, are embellished with foliage and geometric motifs. Their tympana were sculpted in the early 13th century. The tympanum on the right represents the stoning of St. Stephen; the one on the left is particularly striking, depicting the beheading of St. John the Baptist and the death of St. John the Evangelist.

Above these porches, on either side of the Flamboyant rose window, the façade is covered with arcading adorned with statues and topped with gables, rich decoration added in the 14th and 15th centuries. The main entrance, rebuilt in the early 16th century, is itself topped with a huge traceried gable. Its tympanum, badly damaged by the Protestants in 1562, is adorned with a Tree of Jesse, a subject rarely depicted in sculpture.

The arms of the **transept** are flanked with square towers. Their two entrances – *Libraires* ('Booksellers') to the north and *Calende* to the south – are built in the radiating Gothic style and still have their sculpted tympana, statuettes on their arch moulding and quatrefoils on the bases of their jambs, including the famous small bas-reliefs.

The delightful **crossing tower** (13th and 16th centuries) was topped by a 151m-high cast-iron spire in the 19th century – the tallest in France! Flaubert protested against this design, considering it to be the *extravagant attempt of some fantastic brazier*. However, it is in keeping with the building and the hills which surround the city.

2.

3.

1.

## Inside the Cathedral

On entering the cathedral, the visitor is struck by its dimensions: it is 137 m long and 24 m wide, and the nave itself measures 11 m and reaches a height of 28 m up to the vault. Huge compound pillars mark out the eleven bays of the **nave**, which has four levels – the arcades, the bays of the tribunes (although the tribunes themselves were never completed), the triforium and the clerestory. The chapels which open onto the aisles were added in the late 13th century, and some still have their 13th- and 15th-century windows.

Like the nave, the **transept** arms have adjoining aisles but only three levels. The two gable walls, reconstructed between 1280 and 1335, have a series of blind arches at their base topped with gables housing statues; each one boasts a large, radiating rose window above a high bay.

The huge pillars in the crossing bear a two-storey lantern tower with blind arcading and windows which flood

2.

1.
Elevation of the chancel in the cathedral (13th century).

2.
Blind arcading on the first level of the cathedral lantern tower (13th century).

3.
Stained glass from the 13th century depicting the life of the patriarch Joseph, bearing the signature of the Chartres glassworker, Clément (north side of the ambulatory).

3.

the cathedral with light. The octopartite vault above the tower reaches a height of 51 m. The overall impression is one of solidity and harmony.

The **chancel** is the most elegant part of the building. Tall columns crowned with fine capitals decorated with foliage mark out five straight bays and a five-sided apse. As there are no tribunes, the arcades are considerably narrower than those in the nave; in accordance with the Norman tradition, the arches are pointed and the abaci of the capitals are circular. The triforium is composed of delightful tierce-point arcading typical of the 13th century. The clerestory windows were subsequently enlarged, as were those in the nave. Despite the terrible bombing of 1944, the chancel still has some outstanding furnishings, including in particular the 15th-century misericords on the choir stalls which represent craftsmen at work and provide a precious glimpse of life during this period.

The ambulatory has some remarkable 13th-century stained glass windows. One of them, which depicts the legend of St. Julian the Hospitaller, provided the inspiration for one of Flaubert's *Trois contes*; it was a gift from fishmongers. A second window, which tells the story of Joseph, bears the signature: *Clément, glassworker from Chartres, made me.* The tombs of the Norman princes – William Longsword, Richard the Lionheart and Henry the Young King – which are located around the chancel are fine examples of 13th- and 14th-century funeral art; the tomb of Rollo is a 19th-century replica.

The largest of the three chapels in the ambulatory, dedicated to the Virgin Mary, was rebuilt around 1310. As well as its 14th- and 15th-century stained-glass windows, it houses a Louis XIII reredos with a nativity scene painted by Philippe de Champaigne, together with the famous Renaissance tombs of the Cardinals of Amboise and the Archbishops of Rouen and that of the seneschal Louis de Brézé, husband of Diane de Poitiers.

1.

## Around the Cathedral

1.
Opposite the cathedral, the former Finance Office (16th century) has housed Rouen's Tourist Information Centre since 1957.

2.
Façade of the archbishop's palace overlooking the main courtyard (16th and 18th centuries).

2.

The archbishop still lives in the **palace** built by his predecessors to the east of the cathedral. The current palace, dating from the 15th and 16th centuries, was altered in the 18th century.

To the south of the cathedral, on Place de la Haute Vieille Tour and Place de la Basse Vieille Tour, the 1944 bombings spared an unusual building dating from the late Renaissance. It is adjacent to the Cloth Hall and is known as the **Fierte Saint-Romain**; it was built in 1542 by Jean Goujon for the ceremony known as the Privilege of St. Romain. According to legend, this bishop saved Rouen from a fearsome monster, the *Gargouille*, with the help of a man condemned to death, to whom the bishop subsequently granted a pardon. To commemorate this event, the cathedral chapter used to free a murderer each year on Ascension Day. Before being released, the lucky prisoner was led to the location where the miracle was thought to have taken place, where he had to hold aloft to the crowd the shrine or *fierte* of St. Romain. The French Revolution put an end to this privilege.

In front of the cathedral's façade, the former **Finance Office** (*Bureau des Finances*) again bears witness to the Renaissance in Rouen. Built between 1509 and 1542 by the area's tax inspectors (*généraux des finances*), it now

3.

3.
Half-timbered houses, Rue Saint-Romain: the house on the right, with its triple corbelling, was built between 1480 and 1520.

4.
The 'Old House', at 11, Rue Saint-Romain, dates from 1466.

houses the Tourist Information Centre. Its high roof with dormer windows, its large windows which were originally mullioned and its corner niches are all Gothic in style. However, the symmetry, the mezzanine and the décor, which includes arabesques, candelabras and medallions offered by loved ones, are characteristic of the early Renaissance. In the courtyard, which housed the Court of Aids (*Cour des Aydes*), wood was used instead of stone, which was too expensive. The ionic columns and Corinthian pilasters bear witness to the late Renaissance.

The contemporary building to the north of Place de la Cathédrale was constructed on a part of the site of the Hôtel Romé, the seat of Normandy's **Chamber of Accounts** (*Chambre des Comptes*) from the late 16th century to the French Revolution. This fine Renaissance dwelling, built between 1525 and 1550, was destroyed in 1944; only the first two levels of its façade were reconstructed in this modern building, creating wonderful theatrical scenery.

This leads on to the **Rue Saint-Romain**, one of Rouen's most picturesque streets. On the right-hand side, the Albane Courtyard (*Cour d'Albane*) is the perfect vantage point for standing back and admiring the north face of the cathedral. The remains of one of the churches in the early cathedral district were discovered here in 1987. Further along is the 'Old House' (*Vieille Maison*) (1466), the only remaining house on the south side of the street, followed by the Flamboyant Gothic outer gate of the Booksellers' Court (*Cour des Libraires*) and the high north wall of the archbishop's palace. On the gable wall of a large hall which was destroyed in the 18th century, two plaques commemorate the trials in which Joan of Arc was condemned to death in 1431 and rehabilitated in 1456. On the left lie half-timbered houses dating from various periods. The early 16th-century house at number 74 is famous for its triple corbelling, its windows with mouldings and its statuettes. A little further on, at number 70, an Art Nouveau-style house dating from 1902 was the workshop of the Rouen-based wrought iron worker, Ferdinand Marrou.

4.

# The Saint-Maclou District

**Saint-Maclou** Church, which was started in 1436 under the English occupation and completed in 1521, is a masterpiece of Flamboyant Gothic architecture. The originality of the west façade with its five porches arranged in a semicircle is remarkable. These are topped with traceried gables which, together with the gabled towers and the flying buttresses of the nave, form a skilful, subtle whole. The tympanum of the central porch, the only one which is sculpted, represents the Last Judgment. The doors offer outstanding examples of sculpture on wood in the mid-16th century.

The crossing tower bears an elegant stone spire, built in the 19th century to replace a wooden spire which was destroyed in the 18th century.

The exuberance of the exterior contrasts with the stark interior. The church has a nave with three bays flanked with side aisles and chapels. The transept does not extend beyond the aisles, and the chancel, the same length as the nave, has two straight bays leading to a four-sided apse which is surrounded by an ambulatory with radiating chapels. As with other churches in the region, one of the pillars of the chancel stands on the building's central axis. The narrow nave and the absence of capitals accentuates the verticality of the building. Light floods in through the third-storey and chapel windows, and the transept crossing itself is lit by an attractive lantern tower. Beneath the west rose window, a superb Renaissance organ case stands on a platform supported by fine Corinthian columns which bear witness to the talent of Jean Goujon; it is accessible via a sumptuous Flamboyant Gothic spiral staircase.

Around the church, the half-timbered houses in Rue Malpalu, Rue Martainville and Rue Damiette create a particularly picturesque setting.

The district boasts another fine construction, the **Aître Saint-Maclou**, built on land acquired in the 14th century for a cemetery. When this became too small in the early 16th century, three galleries were built around it and their attics were used as an ossuary. In the 17th century, the fourth side was added when the south wing was built; this was turned into a school shortly afterwards. During the following century, the school took over all the buildings. The galleries, which opened onto the cemetery in the same way as a cloister, were closed

1.

2.

3.

4.

1.
Place Barthélemy, entrance of Saint-Maclou Church and 17th-century house.

2.
The Aître Saint-Maclou; west, north and east galleries (early 16th century).

3.
The east façade of Saint-Maclou Church, a masterpiece of Flamboyant Gothic architecture (early 16th century).

4.
View over the chancel and lantern tower of Saint-Maclou Church (15th-16th century).

in, and the roof was raised to accommodate a floor where the ossuary was previously located.

The supporting wall and the columns supporting the upper floor are the only parts made of stone. The rest of the construction is half-timbered. Death is omnipresent here, as befits a cemetery: the carvings on the wall plates and posts represent objects from funeral ceremonies and bones. The carvings on the columns and their capitals were badly damaged during the Wars of Religion in 1559 and 1562. To the west and east, the dance of death consumes in turn the important figures of this world and the clergy, while to the north the sibyls of antiquity, so dear to the Renaissance humanists, proclaim the coming of Christ, triumphant over sin and death.

## From Saint-Maclou to Saint-Ouen

Our next stop is Saint-Ouen Church, via **Rue Damiette** which is lined with delightful half-timbered houses dating from the 13th or 14th (no. 41), 15th (nos. 2 and 16), 16th (no. 7), 17th (nos. 43, 46 and 50) and 18th (nos. 4, 6 and 8) centuries. The central tower of Saint-Ouen can be seen rising up above this fine group of houses. Of the 17th-century Hôtel Aligre (no. 30), all that remains is the stone entrance decorated with a head of Hercules.

Some corbelled houses can also be found in Place du Lieutenant-Aubert; the house at no. 4, dating from the late 15th century, is decorated with statues representing the Madonna and Child and St. Romain.

In Rue d'Amiens, on the left, the **Hôtel d'Etancourt** (no. 97) immediately stands out. This fine stone and timber construction dates from the late 16th and early 17th centuries; its façades are decorated with statues of the ancient deities Venus, Minerva and Juno, together with allegories of the four elements, Water, Earth, Air and Fire. This house was not originally located here; it was transferred to this site in 1967.

1.

1.
Rue Damiette, detail of the entrance of Hôtel Aligre: the head of Hercules covered with the skin of the Nemean lion.

2.
Rue Eau-de-Robec lined with tall houses dating from the 17th and 18th centuries.

2.

3.

4.

3.
Shop sign for a stringed instrument maker on the corner of Place du Lieutenant-Aubert and Rue Eau-de-Robec.

4.
House on the corner of Rue Eau-de-Robec and Rue du Pont-de-l'Arquet: from the 17th century onwards, ground floors were often made of stone and only the upper floors were half-timbered.

Retracing our steps, we head along Rue des Boucheries-Saint-Ouen and then, on the right, **Rue Eau-de-Robec**, which still boasts delightful, curious half-timbered houses dating from the 17th and 18th centuries. These houses are very tall and often have drying lofts where cloth was hung out to dry. Up to the 19th century, textile workers lived in this road, along the River Robec. In *Madame Bovary*, Flaubert referred to the buzz of activity which took place in this street: 'The river, that makes of this quarter of Rouen a wretched little Venice, flowed beneath him, between the bridges and the railings, yellow, violet, or blue. Working men, kneeling on the banks, washed their bare arms in the water. On poles projecting from the attics, skeins of cotton were drying in the air.' For hygiene reasons, the River Robec was diverted in 1939; the stream which has flowed through the street since 1983 is a man-made reconstruction.

At no. 185, the House of the Four Aymon Sons (*Maison des Quatre-Fils-Aymon*), known as the Wedding Hall (*Salle des Mariages*) and built between 1470 and 1480, is the oldest in the street; since 1983 it has housed the **National Museum of Education** (*Musée National de l'Education*). The attractive Renaissance façade which is adjacent to the museum in Rue du Ruissel has elegant stone columns similar to those on the Aître Saint-Maclou.

Rue Eau-de-Robec leads to Place **Saint-Vivien**, where the modest Saint-Vivien Church stands. Built from the 14th to the 16th century, it houses a fine collection of furniture including a superb Renaissance organ case behind its façade. We reach the Abbey Church of Saint-Ouen via Rue des Faulx, with its picturesque 17th- and 18th-century half-timbered houses.

1.

2.

1.
Elevation of the chancel of Saint-Ouen Abbey Church (1318-1339).

2.
The nave and west façade of Saint-Ouen (15th and 16th centuries).

3.
General view of Saint-Ouen from the gallery at the foot of the west rose window, above the large Cavaillé-Coll organ.

## Inside Saint-Ouen Church

Even though the construction of the church spanned more than two centuries, from 1318 to 1549, it nonetheless achieves perfect unity because its successive architects kept to the initial plans. Saint-Ouen can therefore be considered as one of the rare great monuments of radiating Gothic architecture. It is only the tracery on the windows and the base of the pillars in the nave which indicate that it was completed in the 16th century.

The scale of the building is immense: 137 m long, 26 m wide – the nave itself is 11 m wide – and 33 m high. The sense of height is accentuated by the many vertical columns and by the lack of chapels in the nave. The builders pushed the boundaries of Gothic technique to the very limits of what was possible: the pillars are very slender and the walls pierced with huge windows on three levels, providing a wonderful luminosity. The gable walls of the transept arms and the west façade themselves have clerestories topped with beautiful rose windows; the rose window in the north arm of the transept resembles a

3.

five-pointed star like the one in Amiens Cathedral.

The magnificent stained glass windows bear witness to the development of the art of stained glass from the mid-14th century to the early 16th century, being fitted as the church's construction progressed. Scenes from the lives of the saints are depicted in the chapels of the chancel and the side aisles of the nave, while important figures from the Old and New Testaments can be seen in the clerestory windows.

The church houses an exceptional organ made in 1890 by Cavaillé-Coll in the large oak case constructed in 1630 behind the façade.

4.
Saint-Ouen Church, stained glass windows in the Chapel of the Virgin (14th century): the Annunciation and Visitation.

## Stained glass in Rouen

Rouen is today one of the most important cities in France for the quantity, diversity and quality of the stained glass windows preserved in its churches. From the 13th to the 16th century, each period has left its mark:

– warm, brightly-coloured stained glass from the early 13th century, dominated by deep blues and reds (north aisle and ambulatory in the cathedral).

– Bright, elegant pieces from the 14th century where historical scenes from the lives of the saints and important figures are presented on attractive backgrounds of grisaille enhanced by coloured borders and decorative motifs (Chapel of the Virgin in the cathedral and, in particular, the extraordinary chancel in Saint-Ouen Church).

– Fifteenth-century windows with subtle colours which use techniques of perspective (Saint-Maclou Church, the transept in Saint-Ouen Church, the Chapel of the Virgin and north aisle in the cathedral).

– Shimmering designs from the Renaissance with spectacular decorative effects, where, as in the 13th century, colour again covers the whole window (Saint-Godard Church, Saint-Patrice Church, Saint-Romain Chapel in the cathedral and the exceptional Saint-Vincent windows in the Church of Sainte-Jeanne-d'Arc).

Even though in Rouen, as elsewhere, the art of stained glass fell into disuse in the Classical era, it reappeared in the 19th century and numerous churches boast stained glass windows dating from this period. Since the Second World War, some contemporary windows have been added to this fine collection.

4.

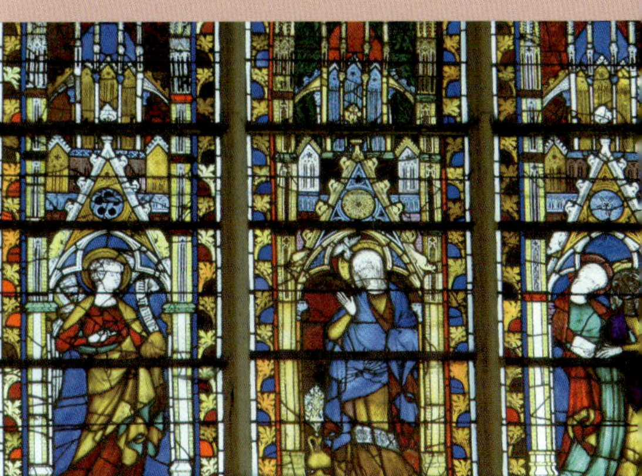

1.

2.

## From the City Hall to the *Gros-Horloge*

Outside Saint-Ouen Church, the façade of the **Hôtel de Bosmelet or Hôtel de Bimorel** (5, Place de l'Hôtel-de-Ville) is particularly striking. This house dates from the mid-18th century and is framed by two half-timbered houses from the late 15th century.

Several routes lead to Rue du Gros-Horloge. The first involves following Rue de l'Hôpital up to the 'Carrefour de la Crosse' (the crossroads formed by Rue Beauvoisine, Rue des Carmes, Rue Ganterie and Rue de l'Hopital), then taking Rue des Carmes up to Place de la Cathédrale. The first part of this route takes us past some fine town houses: **Hôtel Fiquet de Normanville**, dating from the early 18th century (11, Place de l'Hôtel-de-Ville), **Hôtel Jubert de Brécourt**, a fine example of the early Renaissance in Rouen (1, Rue de l'Hôpital) and **Hôtel de Varneville**, also from the early 18th century, which is adorned with an elegant carved pediment (22, Rue de l'Hôpital).

The second route is just as picturesque, taking us past Rue de la République and Place and Rue Saint-Amand, where the remains of a women's abbey stand, including a half-timbered house dating from the 13th century, one of the oldest in Rouen. We join Rue des Carmes via Rue Saint-Nicolas.

**Rue du Gros-Horloge**, the city's most lively street, links Place de la Cathédrale and Place du Vieux-Marché. It has been turned into a pedestrian precinct where visitors can admire the numerous 14th-18th-century half-timbered houses at leisure.

But the road is renowned, above all, for its large public clock, the ***Gros-Horloge***. The late 14th-century mechanism is still in its original location at the top of the neighbouring belfry. The arch which straddles the road and the pavilion on top of it were built between 1527 and 1529 to house the magnificent Renaissance dials, made of sheet iron and lead, painted and gilded, which replaced older dials. A single hour hand shows the time. Below the dials, an opening reveals a bas-relief representing the gods of the days of the week; it changes every day at

1.
Rue du Gros-Horloge is one of the city's oldest streets.

2.
Detail of the dial of the *Gros-Horloge* (16th century).

3.

3.
*Gros-Horloge* (16th century) and belfry (14th century).

4.
The former monks' dormitory at Saint-Ouen Abbey Church (18th century), which became the City Hall in 1800.

4.

noon. The globe above the dials indicates the phases of the moon. The vault of the arch is decorated with a relief depicting the Good Shepherd with his flock; the coat of arms of the city, which bears the Easter Lamb, doubtless symbolising the wool industry, is carved on the keystone of the archivolts.

Before crossing under the arch, stop to admire the former City Hall which stands to the north of the street: this is an imposing construction from the early 17th century, as shown by the huge bosses which decorate its walls.

The austere Gothic **belfry**, built between 1389 and 1398, also houses two 13th-century bells: the *Cache Ribaud* and the *Rouvel* or *Cloche d'Argent* ('silver bell'). The first rang to announce the curfew while the second was an alarm bell. The *Rouvel* called the people of Rouen to revolt in 1382; it cracked in 1904 and is now silent.

At the foot of the belfry, the small house of the governor of the clock stands next to a Louis XV fountain which depicts the love of the god Alpheus for the nymph Arethusa. This very small space therefore boasts a variety of different elements and styles which nevertheless blend together beautifully to create a wonderful overall effect.

1.

# The Law Courts

Follow Rue Thouret, beside the former City Hall, and you will soon arrive in front of the Law Courts (*Palais de Justice*), a superb monument built in the early 16th century to house the *Parlement* of Normandy. The oldest part, located on the west side of the main courtyard (*cour d'honneur*), includes the famous Public Prosecutors' Office (*Salle des Procureurs*) (1499-1509). The work then continued from 1510 onwards with the construction of the central building, the Royal Palace (*Palais Royal*), whose façade is bisected by an impressive octagonal tower. The wing on the east side of the courtyard is neo-Gothic; it was built between 1843 and 1852 to replace a 17th-century building which had collapsed in 1812. A second neo-Gothic wing, parallel to the Public Prosecutors' Office on the west side, was built in 1881 to replace an 18th-century building.

These buildings, whose façades are punctuated by buttresses topped with pinnacles, are a magnificent example of the Gothic style. The Royal Palace in particular is sumptuous, especially the roof. The wall is topped with a huge cornice which supports a Flamboyant Gothic balustrade,

1.
The *Parlement* of Normandy,
now the Law Courts (15th and 16th centuries).

2.
Detail of the south façade of the Law Courts (16th century). The simplicity of the bays with basket-handle vaults on the first floor contrasts with the sculpted decoration on the large windows above them.

3.
Detail of the enlargement of the Law Courts carried out in the late 19th century by the architect Lefort.

2.

above which can be seen a series of basket-handle arches embellished with small pinnacles and statues; the high stone dormer windows are connected to the pinnacles of the buttresses by finely-sculpted flying buttresses.

Inside, two rooms are particularly outstanding. The Public Prosecutors' Office, where Pierre Corneille once pleaded cases before the Water and Forestry Court, is vast, 48m long by 16m wide. It used to be roofed with magnificent panelled pointed barrel vaulting, without tie beams, but this was destroyed by fire in 1944. The room was restored to its former appearance in 1973 with a concrete vault panelled with oak. The second room is the Great Chamber (*Grand'Chambre*), which became the court of assizes. This hall used to boast a splendid Renaissance coffered ceiling which was also destroyed during the Second World War but was fortunately able to be reconstructed in 1988.

In 1976, the remains of a Romanesque building dating from the early 12th century were uncovered in the main courtyard; the graffiti and Hebrew markings indicate that it belonged to Rouen's Jewish community. As the Law Courts were built on the former *Clos aux Juifs*, the Jewish district of Rouen until the Jewish community was expelled by Philip the Fair in 1306, it was firstly thought that this was a synagogue. However, as the building's east wall does not contain a niche for the scrolls of the Torah it seems likely that it was a rabbinic school or the house of the leader of the Jewish community. It is, in any case, the oldest Jewish building to have been discovered in France to date.

3.

# Place du Vieux-Marché

This square is indelibly linked to the memory of Joan of Arc. It was completely transformed under the Second Empire and, in 1979, was again given a new look with the addition of a church dedicated to Joan of Arc, a memorial which had been promised by the French government in 1920, and a covered market. The broken lines of the church's roofs allow visitors to give free rein to their imagination. The architect, Arretche, was concerned only with finding *absolute geometric purity.* The church houses the magnificent stained glass windows from the chancel in Saint-Vincent Church which was destroyed in the 1944 bombings. There could be no better setting than the fine interior of this contemporary church to display this Renaissance stained glass dating from 1520-1530.

On the outside, near to the statue of Joan of Arc (*Statue de la Pucelle*) given to the city in 1926 by Maxime Réal del Sarte, the exact position where she was burnt at the stake is marked by a tall aluminium cross. Half-timbered façades dating from the 16th and 18th centuries, removed from districts which have undergone renovation, have been reassembled on the west side of the square. Everything here symbolises the union of old and new.

The alteration work carried out in 1979 also uncovered the remains of Saint-Sauveur Church, the parish church

1.
Detail of the statue of Joan of Arc sculpted by Maxime Réal del Sartre and given to the City of Rouen in 1926.

2.
Interior of the Church of Sainte-Jeanne-d'Arc, where the stained glass windows of Saint-Vincent Church, which was destroyed in 1944, are housed.

3.
Church of Sainte-Jeanne-d'Arc, stained glass window dedicated to St. Peter (16th century).

1.

## Joan, saint and heroine

Captured by the Burgundians in Compiègne on 23 May 1430 and sold to the English, Joan of Arc was brought to Rouen, the seat of the English Government for occupied France, shortly before Christmas of the same year. The Bishop of Beauvais, Pierre Cauchon, sought refuge in Rouen among his English friends when Charles VII's troops advanced towards his town. He promised to give Joan a *good trial.*
Condemned as a *heretic*, *relapsed heretic*, *apostate* and *idolatress*, she was burnt at the stake on Place du Vieux-Marché, the usual site for executions, on 30 May 1431. She was 19 years old.
She was rehabilitated in 1456 but was only canonised in 1920, when the French Parliament gave her the status of national heroine. This dual recognition was marked on Place du Vieux-Marché with the inauguration of a church on 27 May 1979. This monument, dedicated to the saint celebrated by the Church on 30 May, is extended by a gallery built to honour the memory of the heroine, who is commemorated by the French people on the second Sunday in May (in memory of the liberation of Orléans on 8 May 1429).

2.

3.

4.

4.
South side of Place du Vieux-Marché.

5.
Hôtel de Bourgtheroulde, Aumale gallery: detail of the bas-relief depicting the meeting at the Field of the Cloth of Gold (early 16th century).

5.

of **Pierre Corneille**. The author of *Le Cid* was born and lived near here in a house in Rue de la Pie.

If we head down Rue de Crosne, we arrive at the former hospital (*Hôtel-Dieu*), which has housed the region's prefecture since 1995. The 17th- and 18th-century buildings were the birthplace of **Gustave Flaubert**, whose father was the leading surgeon at the hospital. A small museum is devoted to the writer's memory.

To the south of Place du Vieux-Marché, on Place de la Pucelle, the **Hôtel de Bourgtheroulde** is the oldest stone town house in Rouen. The main residence, located at the back of the inner courtyard (early 16th century), is again of Gothic design. It boasts a polygonal turret and fine dormer windows reminiscent of those at the Law Courts. The bare walls were later embellished with sculpted Renaissance decoration, but this was largely destroyed in the 1944 bombings. On the right, a Classical wing was constructed in place of an older building in the 18th century. It is above all the building on the left, however, which catches the eye. This Italian-style gallery, built between 1520 and 1532, has walls decorated with outstanding bas-reliefs representing the Triumphs of Petrarch and the famous meeting at the Field of the Cloth of Gold between François I of France and Henry VIII of England.

1.

2.

## From Saint-Patrice to Bouvreuil

If we leave Place du Vieux-Marché and take Rue Sainte-Croix-des-Pelletiers, we soon reach Sainte-Croix-des-Pelletiers Church, dating from the 15th and 16th centuries and now used as a conference centre. We then head along Rue des Champs-Maillets, which crosses Rue Lecanuet, and come to **Rue Saint-Patrice**, with its fine town houses dating from the 17th and 18th centuries.

The most famous are **Hôtel d'Arras** (36, Rue Saint-Patrice), built in around 1633, whose façade is embellished with Flemish-style decoration, the 18th-century **Hôtel Mouchard** (42, Rue Saint-Patrice), and **Hôtel de Girancourt** (48, Rue Saint-Patrice), also from the first half of the 17th century, with its fine sculpted decoration.

**Saint-Patrice Church** is a 16th- and 17th-century building with outstanding Renaissance stained glass windows.

A little further on, at 7, Rue du Moulinet, we arrive at **Hôtel de Franquetot** or **Hôtel de Bailleul**; built in the first half of the 17th century, this is one of Rouen's finest town houses.

Crossing Rue Jeanne-d'Arc, we arrive in the Bouvreuil district, with the castle **keep**, the only remaining part of the vast fortress built in 1204 by Philip Augustus. This large cylindrical tower comprises three rooms set one on top of the other and a roof which is a 19th-century reconstruction. Joan of Arc was threatened with torture here on 9 May 1431, but it was in one of the castle's other towers, which has since been destroyed, that she was imprisoned.

1.
Rue Etoupée, house known as Jerusalem (1580) and 15th-century half-timbered house.

2.
Hôtel d'Arras, Rue Saint-Patrice (17th century).

3.
The sumptuous façade of Hôtel de Girancourt and its timber-framed oriel window (early 17th century).

4.
Hôtel Bézuel (17th century), 5 and 7, Rue du Sacre.

5.
Detail of the house known as Jerusalem, Rue Etoupée: a pilgrim on his way to Jerusalem.

3.

4.

## Town houses

Even though wood was clearly the favoured material for house-building in Rouen, stone was also used, much more than was thought to be the case for many years. Numerous town houses in the Saint-Patrice, Saint-Godard and Saint-Ouen districts bear witness to this today, even though they are often hidden away behind their carriage entrance. Some two hundred town houses remain, mostly dating from the 17th and especially the 18th centuries. The oldest, and one of the finest, is the 16th-century Hôtel de Bourgtheroulde in Place de la Pucelle. These mansions were generally the homes of members of the *Parlement* and of the various administrative and law courts, or were owned by rich merchants.

5.

1.

2.

## From Square Verdrel to Square André-Maurois

Not far from the keep, the **Ceramics Museum** (*Musée de la Céramique*), housed in the 17th-century **Hôtel d'Hocqueville** since 1984, has some exceptional pieces from all the periods of ceramic production in Rouen.

Making our way down towards Square Verdrel, we reach the **Fine Arts Museum** (*Musée des Beaux-Arts*) with its large collections of paintings, sculptures and artefacts. Among the most famous works are *Virgin among Virgins* (*La Vierge entre les vierges*) by Gérard David, *Democritus, or The Man with a Globe* (*L'Homme à la mappemonde*) by Vélasquez, paintings by Géricault and numerous impressionist works.

The city's most original museum is undoubtedly the **Ironwork Museum** (*Musée de Ferronnerie*), housed in the former Saint-Laurent Church (16th century). It is named after the collector and donor Le Secq-des-Tournelles and

3.

houses the largest collection of wrought ironwork in Europe.

Just next door, **Saint-Godard Church**, dating from the late 15th century, has fine stained glass windows, the most famous of which is the *Tree of Jesse* (*Arbre de Jessé*) by Arnoult de Nimègue (1506).

To the north of the church, at 20 and 22 Rue Beffroi, stand two fine 18th-century mansions, **Hôtel du Tot de Varneville** and **Hôtel de Coqueréaumont**.

Continuing up Rue Beauvoisine to Square André-Maurois, we reach the **Museum of Antiquities** (*Musée des Antiquités*), housed, along with the **Natural History Museum** (*Muséum d'histoire naturelle*), in a former Convent of the Visitation dating from the 17th century. The museum's fine collections are based on prehistory, ethnography, palaeontology and mineralogy. The Museum of Antiquities boasts outstanding artefacts from the Middle Ages and Renaissance and interesting objects from the Gallo-Roman and Merovingian eras discovered during excavations. All these objects provide an insight into the history of Rouen and its region.

1.
Claude Monet: *Portail de la cathédrale de Rouen, temps gris.*
Fine Arts Museum, Rouen.


2.
Museum of Antiquities: south gallery of the cloister in the Sainte-Marie Convent of the Visitation (17th century).

3.
Hôtel de Coqueréaumont, Rue Beffroi (early 18th century).

4.
Bust, *L'Automne sous les traits de Bacchus.* Le Coq de Villeray factory, around 1730.
Rouen earthenware pottery.


5.
Museum of Antiquities: Madonnas with Child (14th century).

6.
Shop sign of a draper, *L'arbre sec.* Paris, around 1600.
Musée Le Secq-des-Tournelles.


7.
Earthenware in Rouen: decorated plate in shades of red and blue. Guillibaud factory, around 1725.


5.

6.

4.

## Earthenware in Rouen

The first known French earthenware factory was owned by Masséot Abaquesne, who worked in Rouen in the mid-16th century. He supplied several consignments of enamelled tiles for Écouen Castle and for the Bastie d'Urfé castle in Forez, and made a series of apothecary jars. His multi-coloured designs clearly reflect an Italian influence.

The names of Poterat, from the mid-17th century onwards, and Guillibaud and Levavasseur, in the 18th century, particularly stand out in the long line of Rouen earthenware makers.

The decorative theme of embroidery and lambrequin in blue monochrome (17th century), then in blue and red (18th century), made the name of Rouen's glazed earthenware. From the early 18th century onwards, the return of polychrome designs enabled new decorative effects to be produced, with oriental-style motifs, followed by Rococo motifs with genre scenes, floral compositions and cornucopias.

In 1780 Rouen had 25 working kilns, but in the following years the activity of the factories went into decline; the last factory was eventually closed in 1846.

7.

Right:

1.
The cathedral and Saint-Maclou seen between the pinnacles of the Saint-Ouen chancel.

2.
Map of the city centre.

### Panoramic view

**Panoramic photo:**
View of Rouen from the top of Sainte-Catherine Hill.

**Semi panoramic view:**
Half-timbered houses in Rue Malpalu and Place Barthélemy.

**Either side of the panoramic view:**
The cathedral and its spire from the belfry of the *Gros-Horloge*.

Transept of Saint-Ouen Abbey Church (15th century): the rose window of the north arm has a five-pointed star like the one in Amiens Cathedral.


**Editor:** Henri Bancaud
**Editorial coordination:** Caroline Brou
**Graphic design:** attitude.graphique Rostrenen (22)
**Layout:** Editions Ouest-France studio
**Photoengraving:** Micro Lynx, Rennes (35)
**Printing:** Impimerie Pollina - L55078A Luçon (85)
**Publisher no.:** 5630.03.02.08.10
**I.S.B.N.** 978-2-7373-4469-5
**Legal deposit:** March 2008
**Printed in France**
**www.editionsouestfrance.fr**

# Practical Information

## Guided tours of the city

Rouen is a *City of Art and History*; visitors can enjoy tours conducted by accredited heritage tour guides (please contact the Tourist Information Centre).

**1 Rouen Tourist Information Centre**
25, Place de la Cathédrale,
BP 666, 76008 Rouen Cedex 1
Tel. +33 (0)2 32 08 32 46
or +33 (0)2 32 08 36 54.
Fax +33 (0)2 32 08 32 49
www.rouentourisme.com

## Civil and religious buildings

**2 Notre-Dame Cathedral**
Open daily except Monday mornings, 1 January, 1 May and 11 November.

**3 Abbey Church of Saint-Ouen**
Open daily except Tuesdays from 1 April to 31 October.
Open Saturdays and Sundays from 1 November to 31 March.

**4 Church of Sainte-Jeanne-d'Arc**
Open daily except Friday mornings, 1 January, 1 May and 11 November.

**5 Saint-Maclou Church**
Open daily except Mondays and Fridays, 10am-12 noon and 2pm-5.30pm.

**6 Aître Saint-Maclou**
186, Rue Martainville
Open daily.

**7 Gros-Horloge**
Open daily except Mondays
(1 April to 31 October: 10am-6pm;
1 November to 31 March: 2pm-5pm).

**8 Castle Keep (Joan of Arc Tower)**
Open daily except Tuesdays and some public holidays.
Rue du Donjon, tel. +33 (0)2 35 15 69 11

**9 Hôtel de Bourtheroulde**
15, Place de la Pucelle
Inner courtyard open daily.

## Museums

**10 Musée des Beaux-Arts (Fine Arts Museum)** (closed on Tuesdays).
Esplanade Marcel-Duchamp, 76000 Rouen, tel. +33 (0)2 35 71 28 40

**11 Musée de la Céramique (Ceramics Museum)** (closed on Tuesdays).
1, Rue Faucon, tel. +33 (0)2 35 07 31 74

**12 Musée Le Secq-des-Tournelles. Wrought iron craft** (closed on Tuesdays).
2, rue Jacques-Villon, tel. +33 (0)2 35 88 42 92

**13 Musée des Antiquités (Museum of Antiquities)**
Gallo-Roman and Mediaeval archaeology, artifacts from the Middle Ages and the Renaissance (closed on Tuesdays and public holidays).
198, Rue Beauvoisine, tel. +33 (0)2 35 98 55 10

**14 Musée national de l'Éducation (National Museum of Education)** (closed on Tuesdays and public holidays).
185, Rue Eau-de-Robec, tel. +33 (0)2 35 07 66 61

**15 Muséum d'histoire naturelle (Natural History Museum)**
(closed on Mondays and public holidays).
198, Rue Beauvoisine, tel. +33 (0)2 35 98 55 10

**16 Musée Pierre-Corneille**: birthplace of Pierre Corneille.
4, Rue de la Pie, tel. +33 (0)2 35 71 63 92

**17 Musée Flaubert et d'Histoire de la médecine (Flaubert and History of Medicine Museum)**: apartment of the surgeon Achille-Cléophas Flaubert, father of the writer (closed on Sundays, Mondays and public holidays).
51, Rue de Lecat, tel. +33 (0)2 35 15 59 95

**18 Musée de Cire Jeanne-d'Arc (Joan of Arc Waxwork Museum)**: discover the life of Joan of Arc. Audio commentary in four languages (open daily).
33, Place du Vieux-Marché,
tel. +33 (0)2 35 88 02 70

**19 Musée maritime, fluvial et portuaire (Maritime Museum)** (closed on Tuesdays and public holidays).
Espace des Marégraphes – Hangar portuaire no. 13, Quai Émile-Duchemin, 76000 Rouen,
tel. +33 (0)2 32 10 15 51

**20 Musée industriel de la Corderie Vallois (Industrial Museum)** (open 1.30pm-6pm).
185, Route de Dieppe, 76960 Notre-Dame-de-Bondeville, tel. +33 (0)2 35 74 35 35

**21 Pavillon Flaubert**
(entrance hall of Flaubert's house).
18, Quai Gustave-Flaubert, 76380 Dieppedalle-Croisset, tel. +33 (0)2 35 71 28 82

**22 Maison des Champs de Pierre Corneille (Pierre Corneille Museum in the writer's 'country house')** (closed on Tuesdays and Sunday mornings).
502, Rue Pierre-Corneille, 76650 Petit-Couronne,
tel. +33 (0)2 35 68 13 89